AF333289

Muse of the Round Sky

BOOKS BY RICHARD LEWIS

Muse of the Round Sky
Journeys
Still Waters of the Air
Of This World
The Park
The Wind and the Rain
Out of the Earth I Sing
Moon for What Do You Wait?
Miracles
In a Spring Garden
The Moment of Wonder
In Praise of Music

Muse of the Round Sky

Lyric Poetry of Ancient Greece

Selected by Richard Lewis

SIMON AND SCHUSTER · NEW YORK

TEXT COPYRIGHT © 1969 BY RICHARD LEWIS. PUBLISHED BY SIMON AND SCHUSTER, CHILDREN'S BOOK DIVISION. ROCKEFELLER CENTER, 630 FIFTH AVENUE, NEW YORK, NEW YORK 10020.

FIRST PRINTING

SBN 671-65074-2 TRADE   SBN 671-65075-0 LIBRARY
LIBRARY OF CONGRESS CATALOG CARD NUMBER: 79-84136
MANUFACTURED IN THE UNITED STATES OF AMERICA. PRINTED BY PEARL PRESSMAN, LIBERTY, PENNSYLVANIA. BOUND BY ECONOMY BOOKBINDING CORP., NEW JERSEY. DESIGNED BY EVE METZ

The editor and publisher wish to thank the following translators and publishers for the right to use their work in this book:

The poems on pages 14, 18 bottom, 19, 20 bottom, 21, 22 top, 23, 24 middle and bottom, 27, 28, 29, 31, 34, 36 bottom, 42, 48 top, 56, 58, 60, 61, 62, 63, 64 bottom, 68, 74, 76 bottom, 78 top, 79, 84, 89 top, 90 middle and bottom, 91, 93, 95 top and 96 come from *Greek Lyric Poetry*, translated by Willis Barnstone. Copyright © 1962, 1967 by Bantam Books, Inc. All rights reserved. The poems on pages 20 top, 22 bottom, 24 top, 26 bottom, 37, 38 middle and bottom, 40 bottom, 41, 48 bottom, 49, 51 top, 66, 69, 70, 88 bottom, 89 bottom, 90 top and 99, from *Lyra Graeca*, Volumes I-III, translated by J. M. Edmonds, are reprinted by permission of Harvard University Press and the Loeb Classical Library. Poems from *Love Songs of Sappho*, translated by Paul Roche, copyright © 1963, 1966 by Paul Roche, appear on pages 18 top, 35, 43 and 53, and are used with the permission of the New American Library. Poems translated by Dudley Fitts, from *Poems from the Greek Anthology*, copyright © 1938, 1941, 1956 by New Directions Publishing Corporation, are to be found on pages 38 top, 50, 78 bottom and 80, and appear with the permission of New Directions Publishing Corporation. The poem on page 54, translated by Lord Byron, and the poems on pages 67 and 98 bottom, translated by Gilbert Murray, come from *The Oxford Book of Greek Verse in Translation*, edited by T. F. Higham and C. M. Bowra, and are used with the permission of Clarendon Press, Oxford. Poems translated by Kenneth Rexroth, from *Poems from the Greek Anthology*, copyright © 1962 by the University of Michigan, appear on pages 26, 32, 36 top, 85, 92, 94 and 95 bottom, and are used with with the permission of the University of Michigan Press. The poems on pages 40 top, 46, 47, 51 bottom, 59, 64 top, 72, 75, 76 top, 82, 83, 86 and 88, translated by Richmond Lattimore, come from *Greek Lyrics*, copyright © 1949, 1955, and 1960 by Richmond Lattimore, and are used with the permission of Richard Lattimore and the University of Chicago Press.

*To Richard Wooster
who first showed me
the meaning of poetry*

CONTENTS

INTRODUCTION

The past has many secrets. Our knowledge of how people of earlier civilizations lived, thought and felt is often sparse. Even some of the materials of the past are secretive: meanings of words have changed and the context in which they were used is lost; drawings are obscure; the reasons why particular monuments and sculptures or objects were created, unclear.

Yet amidst the secrets, there are a few clues, clues which bring us closer to the past: its people, their lives, and their worlds. The poems in this book, written more than two thousand years ago, are such clues, revealing to us a part of the civilization of ancient Greece—a civilization desirous of giving permanence to itself for the future.

Few people understood the significance of time as did the people of ancient Greece. They were forever aware of its power to transform, to take away and to extinguish all that was alive. Their own lives became a brilliant demonstration of the desire to preserve what was important to them. What-

ever they made, whether it was a vase, a statue, a building, a play or a poem, possessed a strength, a perfection of form and a humanism that seemed able to defy time.

But time has no pity. It chips away at objects and words alike, leaving only fragments. It masks the relevance of deeds once performed. It brings shadows where once there was light.

And so it is with the scars of time upon them that we read and listen to these poems. For some the wound has been deep, and only a line or a phrase is left today. But even in these fragments, small as they are, there is significance and meaning for us.

In these poems there are feelings we recognize: man's response to a season's change; his joy in love; his pain and despair in war; his brooding thoughtfulness about himself; his courage in confronting nature; his sorrow with advancing age; his puzzlement over life and death.

The poets who wrote about these feelings inherited a tradition which insisted that poems communicate and reflect the concerns and experiences of their fellow men. If this had not been so, perhaps many of these lyrics would have lacked real meaning for future generations. The fact that they do communicate to us now, speaking so well of the myriad experiences of our own world, testifies to their success in expressing those basic elements of man's nature which have not changed from century to century.

These poems, then, are a link from the past to the present. They speak for a people who were concerned about the preservation of their own humanity. And for our own time, their concern, as expressed in the words of the Greek poet Alkman, must be our concern as well:

"Counterbalanced against the iron is the sweet lyre-playing."

R. L.

March 1969

Muse of the round sky, daughter of Zeus,
I sing my poems loud and clear to you.

Alkman

PART ONE

All that is born…

WHEN I OPENED MY EYES

Hardly had Dawn
in golden slippers
touched me

Sappho

MORNING

Dawn that ends our sleep
also wakes
the loud nightingale.

Ibykos

DAWN

Dawn was rising full white.

Archilochos

. . . the rising sun straightway filled the great home of the air-walking winds.

Anonymous

THE SUN

Shine on us,
friendly sun.

Folk song

INSTANT

I already hear the flowering spring.

Alkaios

IN MYTHOLOGY

Dew, a child of moon and air,
causes the deergrass to grow.

Alkman

What birds are these which have come from the ends
of the earth and the ocean, wild geese of motley neck
and widespread wing?

Alkaios

FIRST PRINCIPLES

All that is born and grows
comes from water and earth.

Xenophanes

. . . the soft smooth bloom of the fruiting-time.

Alkaios

WINDFLOWER

Bright-shining.

Alkman

ON FLOWERS

Myrtles and violets and yellow cassidonies,
apple flowers and roses and glossy laurel.

Ibykos

24

Traveler in the wilds, do not
Drink this roiled, muddy, warm water,
But go on over the hill where
The cows are grazing, and by the
Shepherds' pine you will find a
Murmuring spring, flowing from the
Rock, cold as snow on the North Wind.

Leonidas

. . . the stormless breath of light winds . . .

Alkaios

WORLD

I could not hope
to touch the sky
with my two arms.

Sappho

SPRING

Spring comes: see where
Graces leave the rose,
how the ruffled sea
smooths into peace,
the water-duck dives,
how the crane soars.
The hot sun burns up
the somber clouds;
fields shine with crops
and olive trees bud.
Everywhere the flood
of swollen grapes
flowers in the vineyard.

The Anakreonteia

THE CRICKET

When sun dazzles the earth
with straight-falling flames,
a cricket rubs its wings
scraping up a shrill song.

Sappho

VACILLATION

The bird flashes back and forth
between the black leaves of laurel trees
and the greenness of the olive grove.

                              Anakreon

RESEMBLING THE BIRDS

In the high branches perch the mottled ducks
and purple cormorants with their sleek throats
and kingfishers of the long wings.

O let my heart always be like the birds
of the purple crest and long wings!

                              Ibykos

The children have put purple
Reins on you, he goat, and a
Bridle in your bearded mouth.
And they play at horse races
Round a temple where a god
Gazes on their childish joy.

Anyte

PART TWO

Love, like a sudden breeze . . .

A GIRL

One day I watched a tender girl
picking some wild flowers.

Sappho

GIRL

A spray of myrtle and beauty of a rose
were happiness in her hands, and her hair
fell as darkness on her back and shoulders.

Archilochos

THE MOMENT I SAW HER

Love
like a sudden breeze
tumbling on the oak-tree leaves
left my heart
trembling

Sappho

Sit down under the high crown
Of this pine, always sounding
In the steady West Wind, and
Here by the splashing current
Pan's pipe will entrance your
Spellbound eyelids.

Plato

TO A HANDSOME MAN

Stand up and gaze on me as friend
to friend. I ask you to reveal
the naked beauty of your eyes.

Sappho

You have made me forget all my sorrows.

Alkaios

NOT OF ITSELF, BUT THEE

Perfume sweet I send you,
    gracing not you but the perfume:
You are yourself the perfume of the perfume.

Anonymous

O ever too delightful one! for many are they
that love thee . . .

Anakreon

For of thee stand I in awe.

Alkman

Here I lie mournful with desire,
feeble in bitterness of the pain gods inflicted upon me,
stuck through the bones with love.

Archilochos

Drink with me, play with me, love with me, be
wreathed with me; be wild when I am wild, and
when I am staid be staid.

Attic Scolia

. . . and she took the golden cup and forthwith
looked at it in wonder.

Anonymous

BRIDEGROOM

What are you, my lovely bridegroom?
You are most like a slender sapling.

Sappho

GOODBYE, BE HAPPY

Goodbye, be happy, bride and groom.

Sappho

The black sleep of night
floods into their eyes

Sappho

PART THREE

...the spur to battle

War is sweet to those who have not tried it. The experienced man is frightened at the heart to see it advancing.

Pindar

Do not against all comers let break the word that is
not needed. There are times when the way of silence
is best; the word in its power can be the spur to battle.

Pindar

EARTHQUAKE

The tyrant's craze for absolute power will soon
demolish his country; already the earth trembles.

Alkaios

. . . these things began, 'tis said, with our fathers . . .

Alkaios

. . . O war, through whom murderous Fear . . .

Alkaios

. . . they cowered like birds at the sudden sight of a swift eagle . . .

Alkaios

We, a thousand, are the murderers of the seven men who fell dead. We overtook them with our running feet. . . .

Archilochos

ON THE DEAD AT THERMOPYLAI

Him who, altering the ways of earth and sea,
Sailed on the land and made his march on the water,
Him the valor of three hundred Spartan spears
    hurled back.

Be ashamed O mountains and sea!

Parmenion

Pain drips

Sappho

WHOM THE GODS LOVE

Whom the gods love die young.

Menander

ALONE

The moon and Pleiades
are set. Midnight,
and time spins away.
I lie in bed, alone.

Sappho

PART FOUR

Yet man seeks...

SEASON OF SONG

Forget the wars.
It is time to sing.
Take out the flute from Phrygia
and recall the songs of our blond Graces.

Clamor of babbling swallows:
it is already spring.

Stesichoros

I am two things: a fighter who follows the Master of
Battles, and one who understands the gift of the
Muses' love.

Archilochos

SHADOWS

Fools and children you are, mankind! You mourn
the dead and not the dying flower of youth.

Theognis

BREVITY

The rose blooms for a brief season. It fades,
and when one looks again—the rose is briar.

Anonymous

THE GODS

The mind of the eternal gods
can not be seen by man.

Solon

SOMEONE, I TELL YOU

Someone, I tell you,
will remember us.

We are oppressed by
fears of oblivion

yet are always saved
by judgment of good men.

Sappho

KNOWLEDGE

The gods did not enrich man
with a knowledge of all things
from the beginning of life.
Yet man seeks, and in time
invents what may be better.

Xenophanes

Oh that it were given to us to open
up the heart of every man, and to read his
mind within, and then to close it,
and thus, never deceived, be assured of a friend.

Anonymous

A PLEDGE

Between us, dear friend,
let there always be truth,
most just of all things.

Mimnermos

. . . who may read with ease the mind of another?

Alkman

THIS DEFILETH A MAN

            My son, you do not see
How everything that dies, dies by its own
Corruption: all that injures is within.
Rust is the poison of iron, moths of wool,
And worms of wood; in you there is a poison
Most deadly, which has made you sick to death
And makes and shall make—envy.

Menander

THE PEOPLE'S SICKNESS

Poverty—our painful and uncontrolled disease—
you maim great peoples with your sister
    Helplessness.

Alkaios

SOCIAL DICTUM

The city is the teacher of the man.

Simonides

God hath laid toils upon all men, one upon this and
another upon that.

Bacchylides

Neighbor is a great thing unto neighbor.

Alkman

I pleased the friend who pleased me.

Anonymous

. . . As for me, when grievous age wears me out, then be it not mine to forget the kindness of such as were my friends of old.

Alkaios

71

Being no more than a man, you cannot tell
    what will happen tomorrow,
nor, when you see one walk in prosperity
    know for how much time it will be.
For overturn on the light-lifting wings of a dragonfly
is not more swift.

Simonides

PART FIVE

*. . . a wash of waves
deep within*

CALM SEA

The calm sea falls dumbly
on the shore
among a tangle of seaweed.

Alkman

DECEMBER

We go through Poseidon's month.
Ponderous clouds sag with water
and furious storms break out
collapsing the rain earthward.

Anakreon

Glaukos, look! The open sea is churning to a wash of waves deep within. A cloud stands upright over the Gyrean cape, signal of a storm, and terror rises from the unforeseen.

Archilochos

Often along the streaming hair
of the gray salt water
they pray for sweet homecoming
won in spite of the sea.

Archilochos

SHIPWRECK

The vessel wavered on the cutting edge
between the stormwinds and the waves.

Archilochos

A DROWNING

They laid down their lives
in the arms of waves.

    Archilochos

EPITAPH OF A SAILOR

I am the tomb of a mariner shipwrecked.
Sail on:
Even while we died the others rode out the storm.

    Theodoridas of Syracuse

A DOUBLE GRAVE

Neither the sea nor land may claim my body.
In this death they share me in equal parts.
The fish devoured all my flesh in the sea,
but my bones were washed up on this cold beach.

Antipatros of Thessalonike

PRIAPOS OF THE HARBOR

Now Spring returning beckons the little boats
Once more to dance on the waters: the gray storms
Are gone that scourged the sea. Now swallows build
Their round nests in the rafters, and all the fields
Are bright with laughing green.
                    Come then, my sailors:
Loose your dripping hawsers, from their deep-sunk
        graves
Haul up your anchors, raise your brave new sails.

It is Priapos warns you, god of this harbor.

Antipater of Sidon

PART SIX

Time's fingers bend
us slowly . . .

I have gone gray at the temples,
yes, my head is white, there's nothing
of the grace of youth that's left me,
and my teeth are like an old man's.
Life is lovely. But the lifetime
that remains for me is little.
For this cause I mourn. The terrors
of the Dark Pit never leave me.
For the house of Death is deep down
underneath; the downward journey
to be feared, for once I go there
I know well there's no returning.

Anakreon

No longer, maiden voices sweet-calling,
          sounds of allurement,
can my limbs bear me up; oh I wish,
          I wish I could be a seabird
who with halcyons skims the surf-flowers
          of the sea water
with careless heart, a sea-blue-colored
          and sacred waterfowl.

Alkman

Not even those who lived long ago before us
and were sons of our lords, the gods,
          themselves half-divine,
came to an old age and the end of their days
without hardship and danger,
          nor did they live forever.

Simonides

SEIZURE

To me he seems like a god
as he sits facing you and
hears you near as you speak
softly and laugh

in a sweet echo that jolts
the heart in my ribs. For now
as I look at you my voice
is empty and

can say nothing as my tongue
cracks and slender fire is quick
under my skin. My eyes are dead
to light, my ears

pound, and sweat pours over me.
I convulse, paler than grass,
and feel my mind slip as I
go close to death.

Sappho

Let this life of worry
Pass by in silence, as
Silent as Time itself.
Live unknown, and so die.

Palladas

Loveliest of what I leave behind
            is the sunlight,
and loveliest after that the shining stars,
            and the moon's face,
but also cucumbers that are ripe,
            and pears, and apples.

Praxilla of Sicyon

ΠΟΛΥΔΕΥΚΕΣ

Blessed is he who has seen these things
        and goes under the ground.
He knows life's end.
He knows the empire given by the God.

Pindar

Remembrance belongs to them that were there.

Alkman

WHO?

Who can be coming to the edge
of my gates
at this black hour of night?

Apollodoros

And the Goddess took and pressed in her hand
the crown-lock of his head.

Alkman

For what once hath happened cannot be undone.

Simonides

HESPEROS

You were the Morning Star among the living.
In death, O Evening Star, you light the dead.

Plato

THE NATURE OF THE UNIVERSE

Everything comes from the earth,
and everything ends in the earth.

Xenophanes

LAMENT

The stars and the rivers
and waves call you back.

Pindar

91

Nothing but laughter, nothing
But dust, nothing but nothing.
No reason why it happens.

Glykon

Time's fingers bend us slowly
With dubious craftsmanship,
That at last spoils all it forms.

Krates

PASSAGE OF TIME

One thousand years, ten thousand years
are but a tiny dot,
the smallest segment of a point,
an invisible hair.

Simonides

. . . about the cool water
the wind sounds through sprays
of apple, and from the quivering leaves
slumber pours down. . . .

Sappho

FULL MOON

The glow and beauty of the stars
are nothing near the splendid moon
when in her roundness she burns silver
about the world.

Sappho

The lines are cast and the nets
      are set and waiting.
Now the tunnies come, slipping
      through the moonlit water.

The Delphic Oracle

PIGEONS AT REST

The hearts in the pigeons grew cold
and their wings dropped to their sides.

Sappho

THE EDGE OF THE WORLD

Last peaks of the world, beyond all seas,
Wellsprings of night, and gleams
      of opened heaven,
The old garden of the sun.

Sophocles

A far-sounding cry of a lyre

Cydias of Hermionè . . . (?)

A NOTE ON GREEK LYRIC POETRY

Greek poetry originated in ritual performances that were a blending
of word, music and dance. One of the first distinct forms to grow out
of this combination was the choral ode *(chorus*—a dancing and sing-
ing performing group; *oide*—a song). The choral odes began as cere-
monial pieces celebrating many of the Greek gods and in time came
to be used for celebrating the excellence of man as well. Soon the
dancing chorus of the odes gave way to the solo song, or monody.
Characteristic of this form were its simplicity and frequent use as
subject matter of the poet's own personal concerns. These elements,
combined with the fact that this type of poetry was usually sung to
the accompaniment of the lyre, created the concept of "lyric" poetry
as we know it today.

ABOUT THE POETS AND SOURCES

Alkaios, a contemporary of Sappho, lived during the sixth century B.C.
He came from Mytilene and was very active in politics.

Alkman lived during the late seventh century B.C. and probably came
from Sparta.

Anakreon, c. 560–490 B.C, was originally from Teos, in Asia Minor.
He settled in Thrace and pursued a career as a professional poet.

The Anakreonteia are an anonymous group of lyrics meant to be imi-
tations of the work of Anakreon.

Antipater of Sidon wrote about 130 B.C.

Antipatros of Thessalonike was writing at the beginning of the Chris-
tian era.

Anyte, who was actively writing around 290 B.C., came from Arkadia,
in the Peloponnesus.

Apollodoros was living during the late sixth century B.C.

Archilochos, c. 680–640 B.C., made his living as a mercenary soldier.
He came from Paros.

Attic Scolia is a song sung during banquets.

Bacchylides, who was writing around 470 B.C., was born at Iulis, in
Ceos. He was a nephew of Simonides.

The Delphic Oracle, early fifth century B.C.: At an ancient shrine of
Apollo, located at Delphi, a male prophet posed questions to a
priestess, or oracle, then interpreted her answers in verse.

Glykon was living *c.* 400 A.D.

Ibycus was living in the second half of the sixth century B.C. He came
from Rhegium.

Krates is represented in the *Greek Anthology,* or *Palatine Anthology,*
a collection of more than 4,000 short poems written between
700 B.C and 1000 A.D

Leonides, who wrote between 55 and 85 A.D., came from Alexandria.

Menander, 324–290 B.C, was an Athenian poet and playwright who wrote over 100 comedies.

Mimnermos lived from the middle of the seventh century B.C. to the beginning of the sixth. He was a citizen of either Kolophon or Smyrna.

Palladas, c. 400 A.D., was a schoolmaster at Alexandria.

Parmenion, c. 50 B.C., came from Thebes.

Pindar, c. 526–446 B.C., was from Thebes. He was employed by different princes and governments to compose choral songs for special occasions.

Plato, 429–347 B.C., was born in Athens. A disciple of Socrates, he was a key figure in the development of Western philosophy.

Praxilla, c. 450 B.C., came from Sikyon.

Sappho, c. 620–550 B.C., came from a noble family and lived her life on the island of Lesbos, at Mytilene.

Simonides, c. 556–468 B.C., was born in Keos. He spent much of his life in Athens, where he served as the poetic voice of Greece during the Persian Wars.

Solon, c. 630–550 B.C., was a soldier, a merchant, a traveler and a poet. He was famous for his social and political work.

Sophocles, 496–406 B.C., was a tragic poet and playwright from Athens, one of the greatest of ancient Greece. He is reputed to have written 123 plays, 7 of which survive.

Stesichoros lived from the last part of the seventh century B.C. to the middle of the sixth. He lived in Himera, in Sicily.

Theodoridas, who lived during the second half of the third century B.C., wrote epigrams. He came from Syracuse.

Theognis, who lived in the middle or latter part of the sixth century B.C. and into the fifth, was from Megara.

Xenophanes, c. 570–480 B.C., wrote much poetry, but is better known as a philosopher. He was born in Colophon.

ABOUT THE ILLUSTRATIONS

The following illustrations appear through the courtesy of the Museum of Fine Arts, Boston:

page 15   A detail from a drawing by Tithonos Painter on a Nolan* amphora (an oval, small-mouthed vase for carrying liquids). Francis Bartlett Collection.

pages 17, 33, 45, 57, 73 and 81.   Upper part of a bearded man, 5th century B.C. Francis Bartlett Collection.

page 21   Unidentified fragment of an amphora.

page 25   Drawing of two girls on a seesaw, on an unidentified vase fragment. Purchased of E. P. Warren.

page 35   A vase fragment, showing the head and arms of a girl dancing. Purchased of E. P. Warren.

page 39   A woman washing her hands; a drawing on the interior of a kylix (a shallow drinking cup). Perkins Collection.

page 55   Soldiers bidding farewell to relatives; detail from a drawing on a Volute* krater (a wide-mouthed vase in which liquids were mixed), attributed to Niobid Painter. Cyrene Excavation Fund and John M. Rodocanachi Fund.

page 61   A detail from a drawing on an Attic* amphora.

page 79   A Boeotian tragic mask, *c.* 400 B.C. Purchased of E. P. Warren.

page 91   A stag, a detail from a drawing on the interior of a kylix, signed by Tleson. Pierce Fund.

page 99   A detail from a drawing by Tithonos Painter, on the same Nolan amphora shown on page 15. Francis Bartlett Collection.

** Refers to the place of origin and/or the style of painting.*

Photographs of two drawings by Exekias, on an Attic amphora in the Vatican Museum, Rome, appear with the permission of Fratelli Alinari, Rome:

page 71   Ajax and Odysseus playing dice.
page 87   The return of Castor and Pollux.

The following photographs by M. Chuzeville are reprinted by permission of the Department of Greek and Roman Antiquities, the Louvre, Paris:

page 31   Zeus and the eagle, drawn on a Laconian* cup, *c.* 550 B.C
page 50   A battle scene, drawn on a Corinthian* krater, *c.* 600 B.C.
page 65   The wounding of Philoctetes, a drawing by Hermonax, on
          a stamnos (a round, small-mouthed vase), 475–450 B.C.

The drawing on page 77 by Exekias, depicting Dionysos in his boat, comes from a drinking cup, 550–525 B.C., and is reproduced with the permission of the Munich Museum.

The frontispiece, which appears through the courtesy of the Greek National Tourist Office, shows three dancing girls on the capital of a column, 4th century B.C., from the Delphi Museum.

** Refers to the place of origin and/or the style of painting.*

SUGGESTIONS FOR FURTHER READING

Barnstone, Willis, *Greek Lyric Poetry*, Introduction. New York: Bantam books, 1962, 1967. Library edition available from Indiana University Press.

Bowra, C. M., *Ancient Greek Literature*. New York: Oxford University Press, 1933. Galaxy paperback, 1960.

Bowra, C. M., *The Greek Experience*. New York: World Publishing Company, 1957.

Hadas, Moses, *The Greek Poets*. New York: Random House, Modern Library edition, 1953.

Hamilton, Edith, *The Greek Way*. New York: W. W. Norton & Company, 1930, 1942; New American Library, Mentor paperback, 1948.

Higham, T. F., and C. M. Bowra, *The Oxford Book of Greek Verse in Translation*, Introduction. New York: Oxford University Press, 1938.

Rose, H. J., *A Handbook of Greek Literature*. New York: E. P. Dutton & Company, Inc., 1960.

Toynbee, Arnold, *Greek Civilization and Character*. New York: New American Library, Mentor paperback, 1953.

INDEX

[*Untitled poems are listed in italic type by their opening words.*]

Richard Lewis has edited several collections of poetry for children, among them Miracles, *an American Library Association Notable Children's Book of 1966, and* The Wind and the Rain, *in which he first collaborated with photographer Helen Buttfield. For their second book,* The Park, *Mr. Lewis wrote the text to accompany Miss Buttfield's photographs.*

Mr. Lewis teaches at Manhattan Country School and the New School for Social Research. He lives in New York City with his wife Nancy and their young daughter Amanda.